THE REVOLUTIONARY WAR

JOHN ADAMS

Anne K. Brown

BLACKBIRCH®
PRESS

THOMSON
— ✦ — ™
GALE

San Diego • Detroit • New York • San Francisco • Cleveland
New Haven, Conn. • Waterville, Maine • London • Munich

For more information, contact
The Gale Group, Inc.
27500 Drake Rd.
Farmington Hills, MI 48331-3535
Or you can visit our Internet site at http://www.gale.com

LIBRARY OF CONGRESS CATALOGING-IN-PUBLICATION DATA

Brown, Anne K., 1962-
  John Adams / by Anne K. Brown.
    p. cm. — (Triangle history of the American Revolution)
Includes bibliographical references and index.
Contents: Introduction: An anxious night in Philadelphia — Crops, college, and court-rooms — Strong men, powerful words — The pursuit of freedom — Struggles of a new nation — The growing pains of government.

  ISBN 1-4103-0257-1 (hardback : alk. paper)
  1. Adams, John, 1735-1826—Juvenile literature. 2. Presidents—United States Biography—Juvenile literature. [1. Adams, John, 1735-1826. 2. Presidents.] I. Title. II. Series: Triangle histories. Revolutionary War.

  E322.B825 2004
  973.04'4'092—dc22

                                                                    2003019631

Printed in United States
10 9 8 7 6 5 4 3 2 1

CONTENTS

PREFACE: THE AMERICAN REVOLUTION

Today, more than two centuries after the final shots were fired, the American Revolution remains an inspiring story not only to Americans, but also to people around the world. For many citizens, the well-known battles that occurred between 1775 and 1781—such as Lexington, Trenton, Yorktown, and others—represent the essence of the Revolution. In truth, however, the formation of the United States involved much more than the battles of the Revolutionary War. The creation of our nation occurred over several decades, beginning in 1763, at the end of the French and Indian War, and continuing until 1790, when the last of the original thirteen colonies ratified the Constitution.

More than two hundred years later, it may be difficult to fully appreciate the courage and determination of the people who fought for, and founded, our nation. The decision to declare independence was not made easily—and it was not unanimous. Breaking away from England—the ancestral land of most colonists—was a bold and difficult move. In addition to the emotional hardship of revolt, colonists faced the greatest military and economic power in the world at the time.

The first step on the path to the Revolution was essentially a dispute over money. By 1763, England's treasury had been drained in order to pay for the French and Indian War. British lawmakers, as well as England's new ruler, King George III, felt that the colonies should help to pay for the war's expense and for the cost of housing the British troops who remained in the colonies. Thus began a series of oppressive British tax acts and other laws that angered the colonists and eventually provoked full-scale violence.

King George III

The Stamp Act of 1765 was followed by the Townshend Acts in 1767. Gradually, colonists were forced to pay taxes on dozens of everyday goods from playing cards to paint to tea. At the same time, the colonists had no say in the passage of these acts. The more colonists complained that "taxation without representation is tyranny," the more British lawmakers claimed the right to make laws for the colonists "in all cases whatsoever." Soldiers and tax collectors were sent to the colonies to enforce the new laws. In addition, the colonists were forbidden to trade with any country but England.

Each act of Parliament pushed the colonies closer to unifying in opposition to English laws. Boycotts of British goods inspired protests and violence against tax collectors. Merchants who continued to trade with the Crown risked attacks by their colonial neighbors. The rising violence soon led to riots against British troops stationed in the colonies and the organized destruction of British goods. Tossing tea into Boston Harbor was just one destructive act. That event, the Boston Tea Party, led England to pass the so-called Intolerable Acts of 1774. The port of Boston was closed, more British troops were sent to the colonies, and many more legal rights for colonists were suspended.

Finally, there was no turning back. Early on an April morning in 1775, at Lexington Green in Massachusetts, the first shots of the American Revolution were fired. Even after the first battle, the idea of a war against England seemed unimaginable to all but a few radicals. Many colonists held out hope that a compromise could be reached. Except for the Battle of Bunker Hill and some minor battles at sea, the war ceased for much of 1775. During this time, delegates to the Continental Congress struggled to reach a consensus about the next step.

During those uncertain months, the Revolution was fought, not on a military battlefield, but on the battlefield of public opinion. Ardent rebels—especially Samuel Adams and Thomas Paine—worked tirelessly to keep the spirit of revolution alive. They stoked the fires of revolt by writing letters and pamphlets, speaking at public gatherings, organizing boycotts, and devising other forms of protest. It was their brave efforts that kept others focused on liberty and freedom until July 4, 1776. On that day, Thomas Jefferson's Declaration of Independence left no doubt about the intentions of the colonies. As John Adams wrote afterward, the "revolution began in hearts and minds not on the battlefield."

As unifying as Jefferson's words were, the United States did not become a nation the moment the Declaration of Independence claimed the right of all people to "life, liberty, and the pursuit of happiness." Before, during, and after the war, Americans who spoke of their "country" still generally meant whatever colony was their home. Some colonies even had their own navies during the war, and a few sent their own representatives to Europe to seek aid for their colony alone while delegates from the Continental Congress were doing the same job for the whole United States. Real national unity did not begin to take hold until the inauguration of George Washington in 1789, and did not fully bloom until the dawn of the nineteenth century.

The story of the American Revolution has been told for more than two centuries and may well be told for centuries to come. It is a tribute to the men and women who came together during this unique era that, to this day, people the world over find inspiration in the story of the Revolution. In the words of the Declaration of Independence, these great Americans risked "their lives, their fortunes, and their sacred honor" for freedom.

The Minuteman statue stands in Concord, Massachusetts.

Introduction:
An Anxious Night
in Philadelphia

★ ★ ★ ★ ★

July 1, 1776, was an anxious day for the members of the Second Continental Congress gathered in Philadelphia. While thunderstorms rumbled above their meeting hall, the delegates, including John Adams of Massachusetts, spent the day in debates. They argued whether the thirteen colonies should declare independence from England.

The idea of independence had been on John Adams's mind for several years, as it had been for many delegates. Those who favored independence had waited patiently until a time that all thirteen colonies might vote together to break from England. Without a unanimous vote, they feared that England would favor any loyal colonies and punish or dissolve those who voted for freedom. The time for the vote had now come.

That morning, John Dickinson, a delegate who was well known for his opposition to independence, gave a lengthy speech that predicted disaster for

John Dickinson argued against the colonies' independence.

the colonies. A vote for independence, he argued, would invite a war with England and, in the end, gain nothing but hardship for the Americans.

The room fell silent, and for long moments, no one arose to debate against him. John Adams waited anxiously for one of his colleagues to speak in favor of independence, but no one stepped forward. He had spoken in favor of separation from England numerous times and knew his arguments well. In the silence of the meeting hall, he arose from his chair and, without notes or a prepared script, began a speech. When three new delegates arrived and begged Adams to repeat what they had missed, he obliged them, carefully recounting his argument for independence. By the time he finished, Adams had spoken for more than two hours. Richard Stockton, one of the new arrivals that day, describing his impressions of Adams, wrote, "He sustained the debate, and by the force of his reasoning demonstrated not only the justice, but the expediency of the measure."

Thomas Jefferson later referred to Adams as "our colossus on the floor with a power that moved us from our seats," and delegate Benjamin Rush called him "the first man in the House." Adams's persuasion was invaluable, yet by the end of the day, several delegates still opposed independence or were undecided.

That evening brought new anxiety to the Continental Congress. British soldiers were already positioned in many towns throughout the colonies,

9

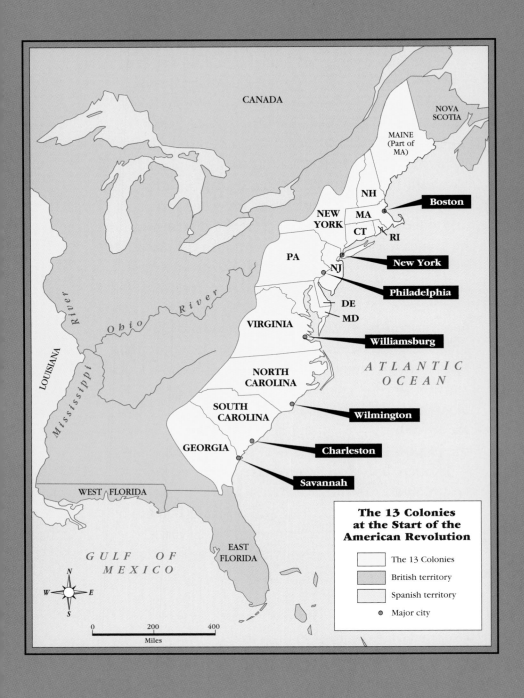

CANADA

NOVA SCOTIA

MAINE (Part of MA)

NH

NEW YORK

MA

CT

RI

Boston

PA

NJ

New York

Philadelphia

DE

MD

VIRGINIA

Williamsburg

ATLANTIC OCEAN

NORTH CAROLINA

SOUTH CAROLINA

Wilmington

GEORGIA

Charleston

Savannah

WEST FLORIDA

EAST FLORIDA

GULF OF MEXICO

LOUISIANA

Mississippi River

Ohio River

N
W   E
S

The 13 Colonies at the Start of the American Revolution

The 13 Colonies

British territory

Spanish territory

● Major city

0   200   400

Miles

but on that July night, word reached Philadelphia that one hundred British warships had been sighted off the coast of New York. To declare independence would mean a war, but to do nothing would leave the colonies in the grip of King George III and British law.

In the taverns and rooming houses filled with delegates on that warm summer evening, conversations were tense. Many delegates had been influenced by Adams's speech that morning, but four colonies opposed independence, and the votes of some delegates remained in question. An avid supporter of independence from Delaware was missing. No one knew if enough votes would swing in favor of independence by morning.

At nine o'clock on the morning of July 2, just as the doors to the meeting room in the State House were about to be closed, the missing delegate from Delaware arrived, spattered with mud after riding eighty miles on horseback during the night. The chairs of two delegates who opposed independence sat empty. The meeting was called to order as new storm clouds billowed above Philadelphia. John Adams, Thomas Jefferson, and the rest of the delegates nervously prepared for the vote that might signal a new future for the American colonies.

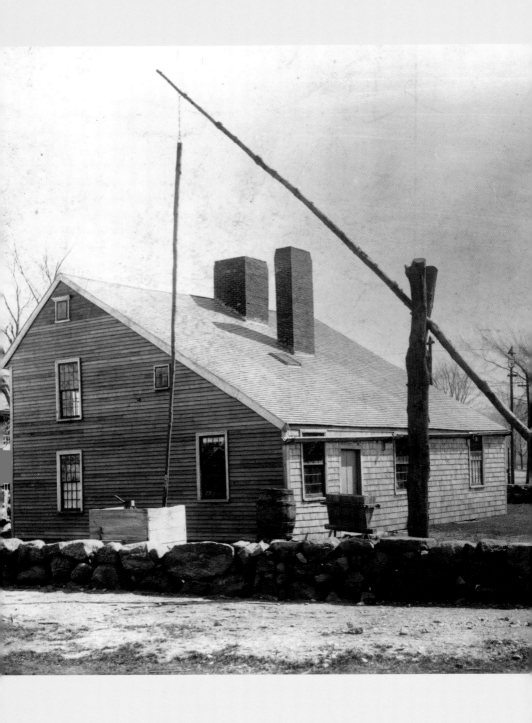

Chapter 1

CROPS, COLLEGE,
AND COURTROOMS

B y the time John Adams became a signer of
the Declaration of Independence in 1776, his
homeland had changed dramatically since his
boyhood. When Adams was young, the United
States did not yet exist. John Adams grew up in
Massachusetts, which was a colony that belonged
to England. In the early 1700s, the lands that
eventually became the eastern United States
belonged to either England or France.

OPPOSITE: John Adams, his wife, and their children lived in this house
in Braintree, Massachusetts, near the farm where Adams grew up.

As residents of Massachusetts during these years, Adams and his family considered themselves British subjects in all ways. They obeyed British laws, used British money, and enjoyed British rights and responsibilities. King George II reigned in Britain, and residents of Massachusetts, as well as other English colonies, regarded him as their ruler.

Early in John Adams's life, however, colonists became frustrated. They felt that British laws did not treat them fairly and that the king's taxes were too burdensome. The colonists began to resent the British government and wished to govern themselves. About the time Adams became an adult, a revolution was brewing. John Adams, with his keen intellect, reputation for honesty, and deep sense of fairness, became a powerful leader at the heart of the American revolt. His speeches and writings greatly influenced the opinions and actions of his fellow colonists. Adams became one of many important men and women who helped break the king's grip on the colonies and create the new United States of America.

The Family Farm in Braintree

Nearly one hundred years after his great-great-grandparents emigrated from England to Massachusetts, John Adams was born on October 30, 1735. His birth took place in his parents' farmhouse, and John was named after his father.

The Adams farm lay in Braintree, Massachusetts, about a mile from the Atlantic Ocean and a little less than ten miles from Boston. The Adamses were well-known and respected in the community of about two thousand residents. Although the family was never wealthy, its members were known as hardworking, honest, pious people.

John's father, like all the Adams men, was a farmer. During the cold winter months when the farm fields were covered in snow, John's father supplemented the family's income by making shoes in the farmhouse. The elder John Adams was best known, though, for his role as a deacon in the local church. Young John observed that the public business of Braintree never took place without his father being consulted.

The Adams family lived in a small but sturdy saltbox house situated on about fifty acres of land. The house had a massive chimney in the center and three rooms on the first floor. The second floor had two bedrooms that were terribly cold in the winter and blazing hot in the summer.

The family grew but never moved from the farm. When John was three, his brother Peter was born. Six years later, baby brother Elihu joined the family. All the boys learned to help around the farm as soon as they were old enough. Even before their children were born, however, John's parents planned to send their oldest son to college.

Lessons to Be Learned

John's mother and father taught him to read when he was very young. At age six, he attended a dame school—a small group of children taught in the home of a neighborhood teacher. When John was old enough, he was sent to school in Braintree to prepare for college. He learned to read and write Greek and Latin in addition to learning the basic subjects. At that time, students were accepted into college only if they could demonstrate their mastery of Greek and Latin.

Because they had such high hopes for his future, John's parents worried a great deal about him. John was happiest when he was outdoors, and he spent many hours visiting the beach and playing in the woods and creeks around Braintree. John loved to sail homemade boats, shoot marbles, and fly kites. He swam in the summer and skated on frozen ponds and creeks in the winter. He disliked studying, and his parents wondered if he would ever be accepted into college.

John despised the Latin School and often sneaked out of his classes. When he was around thirteen years old, he told his father that he wanted to quit school because he wished only to be a farmer. His father insisted that John remain in the Latin School.

When John was fourteen, he again begged his father to remove him from the Latin School. Instead, he wished to study with a teacher named Joseph Marsh, whose school was only two doors away from the Adams farm. John's father made the arrangements the same day. Young Adams got along well with Marsh, and his work improved.

John Adams attended Harvard College in Cambridge, Massachusetts, where he developed a love of books.

The Fears and Thrills of College

When Adams was fifteen years old, Joseph Marsh decided that his student was ready to apply to college. The only such institution in North America was Harvard College in Cambridge, Massachusetts, about ten miles away. The first step was for John to take entrance examinations and be interviewed by the faculty. Joseph Marsh planned to accompany John to Cambridge on horseback.

On the morning they were to leave for Harvard, however, Marsh fell ill and could not make the journey. Young John Adams had to travel alone. He was so terrified of the trip and the exams that he almost turned back, but the idea of facing his father's disappointment was even more frightening, and Adams forced himself to continue to Cambridge. To his surprise, he performed well in his exams and

17

interviews, and even found the Harvard faculty to be kind. That day, he was accepted into Harvard with a partial scholarship. In his diary, he wrote, "I was as light when I came home, as I had been heavy when I went."

His college years proved to be a turning point for Adams. Acceptance into Harvard gave him a sense of accomplishment. He began to enjoy his studies despite a rigorous schedule. Students awakened before sunrise and attended classes all day with only a short lunch break. Homework and studying were done after dinner.

Adams could sense the changes taking place in himself. In his autobiography, he wrote, "I soon perceived a growing Curiosity, a Love of Books and a fondness for Study." Although he had never liked to read, Adams even began to enjoy poetry while at Harvard. Later in life, he became an avid collector of books and never left on a journey without a favorite book to keep him company.

A Career Decision

In Adams's day, students who attended college chose their careers around the time of their graduation. Most college graduates sought further education to become lawyers, doctors, or clergymen. A few went into business or became teachers. Adams faced the most difficult decision of his life. His father, whom he respected and admired, hoped that John would become a member of the clergy. During his years at Harvard, however, Adams had enjoyed the study of law, and his friends had encouraged him to become a lawyer because he reasoned well and was an excellent public speaker.

The decision weighed heavily on Adams. He wished to make his father proud, and Adams's father had sold several acres of the family farm in order to pay the tuition at Harvard, which gave Adams a sense of obligation to his father. On the other hand, the study of law greatly appealed to Adams. He enjoyed the mental challenge that it brought, and he realized that a law career could allow him to live quite comfortably.

★

In the early 1750s Thomas Paine worked as an apprentice in his father's corset shop in England.

★

Adams recorded the turmoil over this decision in his diaries. He wrote that he longed for fame and recognition as a great man of intelligence and integrity. At the same time, his Christian morals stressed modesty. He worried that he could not achieve fame in the courtroom while remaining true to his faith.

This decision plagued Adams for several years. Immediately after his graduation from Harvard in 1755, he accepted a job as a teacher. Although he had no desire to remain a teacher, the job would give him time to make his career decision.

Teacher and Student

Adams's teaching position was in Worcester, Massachusetts, a town slightly smaller than Braintree about fifty miles west of Boston. He found the town to be dreary, and he missed the

19

Many of the more than one thousand letters John Adams wrote to family and friends have survived and provide details of his thoughts and the Revolutionary War.

excitement of Harvard. Adams quickly grew frustrated with the drudgery of his classroom. Extreme boredom eventually forced him to make a decision. In August of 1756, just before he turned twenty-one years old, Adams decided to become a lawyer. He made arrangements to study with James Putnam, the most important attorney in Worcester.

The next two years were difficult for Adams. He kept his teaching job during the day and studied law in the evening. He had little free time and no time at all to meet young men and women his own age. According to Adams's diaries, his only social affairs were invitations to tea or dinner at the homes of some important families in Worcester. He had little opportunity to relax with friends as he had done at Harvard.

War Over the American Colonies

Soon after Adams began his study of law, he became more comfortable in his abilities, and his confidence in his choice of career grew. In 1757, however, Adams wondered whether he should abandon his studies and enlist in the army to fight in the ongoing war in America.

The war had broken out in 1754 while Adams was still a student at Harvard. France and Britain were fighting over control of the New World. Since both countries received help from different Native American tribes, the war became known to British subjects as the French and Indian War.

Several times, Adams wrote in his letters and diary about his desire to become a soldier. His father and grandfather had served as military officers, and Adams sometimes felt that he should continue the family tradition. Also, war offered opportunities for recognition: War heroes were often honored with monuments, and sometimes entire towns were named for them.

Adams at first ignored the fact that other young men in similar circumstances—college graduates just beginning their careers—almost never joined

21

The Paper Trail of John Adams

★ ★ ★ ★ ★

Many documents survive from the days of the Revolutionary War, but no individual left a written record that compares to the writings of John Adams. As an adult, Adams hardly went a day without writing a letter or scribbling in his diary. The majority of these documents survive, and they allow for detailed study of the private world of John Adams.

As compared to Adams, the surviving letters and papers written by George Washington and Thomas Jefferson are few. George Washington's wife burned all of his letters after he died. Thomas Jefferson was married for only ten years when his wife died, so their time for correspondence was relatively short. John and

the army. More typically, farmers and laborers went to war. Therefore, a decision by Adams to join the army would have been unusual.

Adams decided not to join the army, but this decision plagued him privately for decades. He expressed regret in his diaries, but he also realized that service to his country could come in many forms, not only in the army. He took inspiration

Abigail Adams, on the other hand, wrote more than one thousand letters to each other during their fifty-four-year marriage. In their private missives, the brave colonists who became president and first lady wrote to each other of their hopes and fears, their worries and joys.

In addition, John Adams rarely restrained himself while writing. He recorded his moods and anxieties, his anger and his triumphs, whereas Jefferson and Washington normally kept their correspondence free of personal feelings. Adams frequently analyzed his own behavior in his diaries, as in an entry from December 1772 in which he scolded himself for his remarks after a heated discussion with an English gentleman: "I cannot but reflect upon myself with Severity for these rash, inexperienced, boyish, raw, and aukward Expressions. A Man who has no better Government of his Tongue, no more command of his Temper, is unfit for every Thing, but Childrens Play, and the Company of Boys." These comments provide remarkable insight into the internal struggles of this famous American.

As a result of his numerous diaries and letters, as well as his autobiography, more is understood about John Adams's personality and ambitions than any other person of his era.

from the Roman poet Ovid, whom he quoted in his writings: "I am outstanding in intellect. My mind is superior to my hand. All my force is in my mind."

Pursuit of the Courtroom Dream

In August 1758, Adams finished his law studies. He had impressed many people in Worcester and was offered a position as town registrar, an official who created and filed documents and records. Adams turned down the job, and instead, he moved back to his parents' home in Braintree.

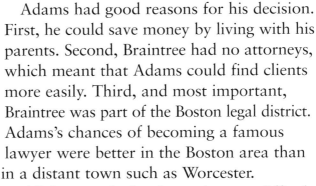

In 1759 George Washington married Martha Custis, who was the wealthiest widow in Virginia.

Adams had good reasons for his decision. First, he could save money by living with his parents. Second, Braintree had no attorneys, which meant that Adams could find clients more easily. Third, and most important, Braintree was part of the Boston legal district. Adams's chances of becoming a famous lawyer were better in the Boston area than in a distant town such as Worcester.

The establishment of a legal practice was difficult. A new lawyer first had to be admitted to the bar— an organization of lawyers that screened its members for their qualifications and then monitored their practices. In the autumn of 1758, Adams met with a prominent Boston attorney named Jeremiah Gridley. He quizzed Adams for several hours about his studies and was so impressed that he personally began the process of Adams's admission to the bar. On November 6, 1759, after a full year of rigorous study, John Adams was admitted to the bar during an official ceremony in Boston. Only a week earlier, he had celebrated his twenty-fourth birthday.

Adams's next challenge was to build a reputation as a successful trial lawyer so he could attract clients. In his first case, he represented a man whose crops had been trampled by two runaway horses. Although Adams understood the law fully and was well prepared, he lost the case because he

24

had omitted a few phrases in one of his papers. Humiliated and furious with himself, he worried that he might never make a living as a lawyer.

Courtship and Marriage

Adams continued to work hard, study, and gain more clients. In the fall of 1760, he was thrilled to win his first case in front of a jury. He soon won more cases, and his confidence grew. As word of his victories spread, he gained the respect of some important lawyers around Boston.

Adams's enjoyment of his success was interrupted in 1761, when his father died during a flu epidemic. Adams wrote about his father: "He was the honestest Man I ever knew. In Wisdom, Piety, Benevolence and Charity In proportion to his Education and Sphere of Life, I have never seen his Superiour." At times, Adams was so upset over his father's death that he could barely leave his home. Gradually, though, his grief lessened, and he returned to his work and other activities.

The year 1761 also held happier times for Adams. That year, at the age of twenty-six, he became acquainted with seventeen-year-old

Abigail Adams advised her husband throughout their marriage.

Abigail Smith. Adams soon began to pay frequent visits to the Smith home, even though he had always felt uncomfortable and shy around women. After a little more than a year, Adams was deeply in love, and Smith was hinting at marriage.

A few years later, on October 25, 1764, John Adams and Abigail Smith became husband and wife. Adams had inherited one-third of his father's land, and the couple moved into a new house next to Adams's boyhood home.

★

In 1765, John Paul Jones, known as John Paul, was a third mate on a British slave ship.

★

New Hope for the Future

At the age of twenty-eight, John Adams had a new wife and a growing legal practice. Life in the American colonies had quieted after Great Britain won the French and Indian War in 1763. France signed a treaty that gave England control of all the American colonies. Most important, the fighting was over.

For John Adams, these were wonderful years. He and Abigail were thoroughly happy in their marriage. Their joy increased when Abigail gave birth to a daughter on July 14, 1765. She was named Abigail after her mother, but her parents and relatives called her Nabby.

Adams's workload, reputation, and fame all grew during these years. His legal work often required him to spend days or weeks away from home. Even though Adams missed his family terribly, his travels allowed him to visit many cities and towns, meet important people, and gain an understanding of the colonists' concerns and desires. As a result, he wrote a number of articles for the Boston Gazette and other newspapers. Adams was soon widely known as an accomplished writer and speaker.

As Adams traveled, he could see trouble brewing in the colonies. During the French and Indian War, the colonists had begun to think of themselves as Americans rather than British subjects. More than ever, they wanted to govern themselves, and they resented the laws passed by the king of England.

The Americans were also forced to adjust to a new king, which made people feel even more uncertain and unsettled. In 1760, King George II died. His grandson, George III, took the throne at the age of twenty-two. Although he was considered an unwise man and a poor ruler, he controlled the American colonies whether his subjects there liked it or not.

Britain levied a number of taxes on the colonies that people felt were unfair. The king also insisted that laws be enforced by judges and agents sent from England, rather than Americans. The colonists complained bitterly about the king's laws and began to look for ways to take control of their own lands.

Among the people who spoke out about these problems was the lawyer named John Adams. He wrote articles about how to solve these problems, what form of government was best, and the rights of the colonists. He spoke out against the unfairness of the king's laws. Adams was soon recognized as a man of great intelligence, ideas, and vision for the future.

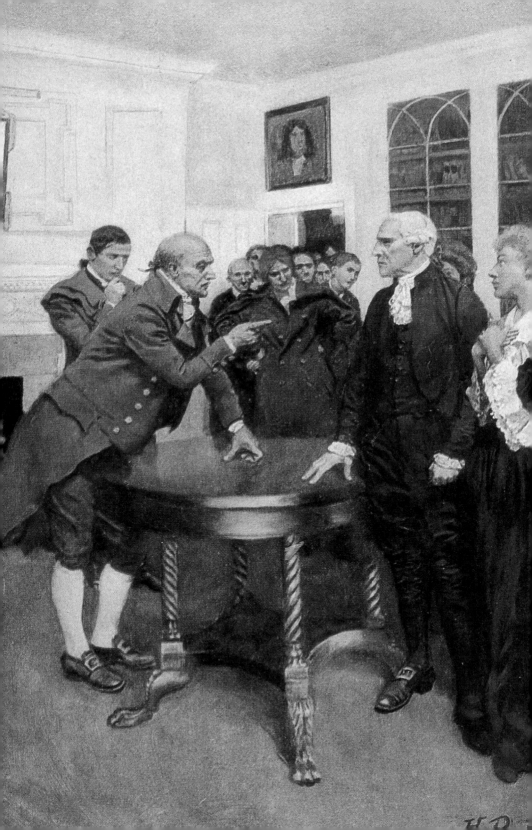

Chapter 2

STRONG MEN, POWERFUL WORDS

John Adams could feel the unrest growing in the American colonies in the 1760s, and he observed many men who tried to gain personal power through the political upheaval. In 1763 he made a public statement about some of the dirty politics in the colonies by publishing seven articles in the Boston newspapers. Such an act was risky; the articles criticized some of Adams's colleagues. To protect his reputation, Adams wrote in the style of an uneducated colonist, with poor spelling and grammar, and signed his work "Humphrey Ploughjogger." Under this pen name, Adams was free to poke fun at certain prominent men for their political maneuvering and to call for fairness and honesty among those with political power.

OPPOSITE: Samuel Adams (left), John Adams's cousin, formed the Sons of Liberty to protest British rule of the colonies.

The names of Boston merchants who continued to import British goods despite a boycott appeared in this edition of the *Boston Gazette*.

At the same time, Adams published a number of serious articles in the *Boston Gazette*. Instead of signing his name to these scholarly essays, Adams signed them simply as "U." In them, he mused about the ideal form of government. He concluded that government needed a balance of powers, not the freedom to do as it pleased. Further, it had to fairly represent all the people that it governed. Adams also believed that a fair government would provide safeguards against personal and political corruption.

By publishing essays in two different styles written under two different pseudonyms, Adams reached a broad audience. Readers who might have found one author too dry or too silly might have read the other. In one article that Adams signed "U," he even complimented the advice given by Humphrey Ploughjogger.

Meanwhile, Britain suffered from financial difficulties because of the many wars it fought in the 1700s, including the French and Indian War. It needed money, and King George decided to tax the colonists. In his opinion, the colonists had benefited from the French and Indian War, so they should help pay the costs. In reality, the war had forced France out of the New World and given Britain control of America. The colonists saw little benefit to themselves from the French and Indian War.

Instead of asking the colonists to help Britain recover from its financial troubles or explaining that taxes were needed to pay for the wars, the

Under the Stamp Act, colonists had to affix stamps like these to every printed document as proof that they had paid the required tax.

John Adams

British Parliament simply invented several taxes for Americans to pay. The first was the Revenue Act of 1764, known to Americans as the Sugar Act. It placed a duty on sugar and molasses, as well as coffee, indigo, wine, silk, and fabrics. The colonists were upset by the amount of the taxes, but they were more angry that the taxes were levied without Americans having a representative in the British Parliament to speak on their behalf.

The Stamp Act Ignites the Colonies

In May 1765 Americans learned that Parliament had passed the Stamp Act, which was to take effect that November. This law meant that every court document, newspaper, receipt, and pamphlet was required to carry a stamp showing that its tax had been paid. The law included many other kinds of documents, as well as almanacs, calendars, decks of playing cards, and pairs of dice. News of this law infuriated many people, but especially businessmen, newspaper publishers, lawyers, and others who made their living by handling or printing documents.

Riots broke out all over the colonies in response to the Stamp Act. The homes of several British officials were damaged. Some colonists organized boycotts—people refused to buy merchandise from England as a means of hurting British trade. Americans were angry that once again, Parliament taxed them but denied them a voice in government. To make matters worse, the taxes were expensive.

Adams Reacts to the Stamp Act

The Stamp Act served an unparalleled purpose for Americans in 1765—it united them in a common cause. More than ever, it made them think of America as separate from Great Britain. John Adams recorded this transition in his diary: "That enormous Engine ... for battering down all the Rights and Liberties of America, I mean the Stamp Act, has raised and spread, thro the whole Continent, a Spirit that will be recorded to our Honour. ... The People, even to the lowest ranks, have become more attentive to their Liberties, more inquisitive about them, and more determined to defend them." For the rest of his life, John Adams remembered the Stamp Act as the true beginning of the Revolution in America.

In response to the Stamp Act, Adams published two documents that historians regard as some of the most important work of his young life. The first was a four-part essay called "A Dissertation on the Canon and the Feudal Law," published anonymously in the *Boston Gazette*. It praised the men and women who emigrated to America in search of religious and political freedom. Adams honored the sacrifices of those who gave up the comfort of their homelands and struggled to build a new life. He also voiced concern that the colonists might face war and other hardships in order to maintain their liberties.

The other important paper that Adams created was a set of instructions that was delivered to

Braintree's representative to the Massachusetts legislature. This document detailed the opinions of Braintree's residents so their representative would know how to debate issues surrounding the Stamp Act. Adams's words were strong and direct, and they laid out the reasons that Braintree despised the Stamp Act. Before long, forty other towns copied the document for their own representatives because it captured their attitudes so precisely. Adams gained fame for this well-crafted composition.

The Stamp Act Is Repealed

Although John Adams's reaction to the Stamp Act was thoughtful and rational, protests in many places became violent. The Stamp Act protests terrified the British agents who were appointed to collect taxes and issue stamps; some were so fearful of harm to their families or homes that they resigned their positions. On November 1, 1765, the Stamp Act became law, but stamps were unavailable since no one could be found to issue them. Soon, harbors and courts were closed since their paperwork was not legal without the stamps. Lawyers such as John Adams could not work, goods could not enter or leave the American harbors, and newspapers could not be published.

King George and Parliament knew that the colonists were angry about the Stamp Act, but they refused to end it. In the spring of 1766, however, the British Parliament realized that trade with the colonies had slowed. The Stamp Act was not generating the amount of money that Britain had hoped for, and the slow trade meant new financial problems. Parliament finally repealed the Stamp Act. The Americans were overjoyed, and throughout the colonies, celebrations took place in honor of this victory.

The Colonies Are Quieted

Following the repeal of the Stamp Act in 1766, the colonies became peaceful. John Adams observed, however, that American thinking remained changed. In elections for government positions, candidates who favored King George and his control of the colonies lost their contests, while candidates who opposed the Stamp Act were victorious. John Adams himself was elected to a position on the Braintree board of selectmen.

Adams's fame as a lawyer was growing. His family was living comfortably on the farm in Braintree. His legal profession, however, frequently kept Adams away from home. Like most lawyers, he visited many towns around Boston depending on the schedule of the court. Travel was slow, almost always on horseback. Adams was even away from home when his second child, John Quincy, was born on July 11, 1767. In his diaries, Adams often noted how badly he missed his family.

In April 1768, John Adams made the difficult decision to move his family to a rented house in Boston. He worried that life in the grimy city would harm their health, but with a home nearby,

This woodcut depicts colonists after they set fire to a British boat. Colonial protests became more violent as the British government imposed new taxes.

Adams could attend the courts and see his family more often.

Adams's move to Boston coincided with a new crisis in the colonies. The Townshend Acts, passed in mid-1767, placed an import duty on lead, paint, glass, paper, and tea. At first, the colonists reacted with discussions in the legislatures and numerous articles in newspapers. By the summer of 1768, though, Bostonians were taking part in public demonstrations. One of these turned violent, and a boat belonging to a British official was destroyed.

Patriotic Decisions

That same summer, John Adams faced an important career decision. Jonathan Sewall, a lawyer who worked for the governor of Massachusetts, offered Adams a job as advocate general in the court of admiralty, one of the highest legal positions in the province. It would mean immediate fame and a handsome salary.

36

The job, however, would make Adams an employee of the British government. His appointment required approval by King George—an extremely high honor that would also put him in line for greater positions—but Adams would then be on the side of the British. His conscience did not allow him even to consider the offer; to maintain his loyalty to American rights and freedoms, he turned down the post immediately.

As the summer of 1768 wore on, public demonstrations against the Townshend Acts continued. Some of them were led by John Adams's cousin, Samuel Adams, and a group he had formed called the Sons of Liberty. On August 1, 1768, the colonists were successful in establishing another boycott of British goods. The residents of several colonies refused to buy British paper, tea, building materials, and other items. Britain lost money as it had during the Stamp Act crisis. In April 1770, in response to the enormous trade losses, Parliament repealed the import duties on all goods except tea.

★

In 1770 King George III celebrated ten years on the throne.

★

The year 1770 had started badly for the Adams family. In February, the Adams's baby daughter, Susanna, a little more than a year old, died as a result of illness. The loss was devastating to the Adamses, especially Abigail, who was again pregnant at the time of Susanna's death. On May 29, 1770, joy returned to the family when she gave birth to a healthy son. He was named Charles, and his arrival and good health helped to cheer his parents.

37

The Boston Massacre

Baby Charles was born shortly after another crisis in Boston. On March 5, 1770, a rowdy crowd of several hundred people formed in the streets of Boston. The mob surrounded a group of eight British soldiers and their commander, and many people threatened or yelled insults at the patrol. The situation grew tense, the soldiers became fearful, and a few people in the crowd dared the soldiers to shoot. The commander never gave the order to fire, but the soldiers began to shoot, and five people were killed. The captain hurried his men away, and the crowd dispersed out of fear.

The event became known as the Boston Massacre, and several colonists, including the Sons of Liberty, used the event to illustrate the evils of British rule. Even though the British soldiers were outnumbered by the threatening crowd, the event was sometimes distorted to make the soldiers appear to be brutal murderers. The soldiers faced a trial to determine their guilt or innocence. The captain was desperate to find a lawyer to defend himself and his men at trial. When he begged John Adams to take the case, Adams agreed without hesitation.

The case placed Adams in a precarious position. By defending the soldiers, he might have seemed loyal to Britain instead of to his fellow colonists. If he won the case for the hated soldiers, Adams might have appeared to favor the soldiers over the colonists who were killed. There was the very real chance that taking the case would permanently damage his reputation, cause him to lose clients, and ruin his chances for future success. All of Adams's years of reading and learning about the law, however, made him a staunch believer in every person's right to a fair trial. His conscience would not allow him to turn away the British soldiers who desperately needed a lawyer.

In 1770 British soldiers killed five people in the Boston Massacre. Adams faced criticism when he agreed to defend the soldiers at their trial, but maintained his reputation for integrity.

An Unpopular Task

For a time, rumors and gossip circulated about Adams's motives for taking the case. Some even suggested that he had accepted a bribe. The trials were postponed until Boston's emotions about the events settled down. In October 1770, Adams successfully defended the captain in court, and his client was set free. In December 1770, the eight soldiers faced the court. Six of them were set free, while the remaining two were convicted of manslaughter and received minor penalties.

39

After the verdicts, some angry letters were written in the Boston newspapers about John Adams and the trials, but no public demonstrations were staged. Adams lost some clients, but neither his practice nor his reputation were destroyed. Adams's integrity was intact, and in the end, he gained respect for his part in this ordeal.

Birth of a Political Career

Despite the gossip and ill will about the trials of the British soldiers, Adams was elected as a representative to the Massachusetts legislature in 1770. He won by a large margin that reflected widespread respect for him throughout Boston. In his journal, he noted that he was pleased to have built a reputation of honesty and integrity that carried him through such an unpopular case.

Adams was honored to be elected to the legislature, but the position meant less time at home and less time for his legal work, which also reduced his income. John and Abigail Adams realized the importance of his position in the legislature, however. With a revolution in progress, Adams wished to serve as a representative to help protect the rights of the colonists. In order to gain liberties for the colonies and prevent unfair treatment by the king, Adams and his wife agreed that they could survive any difficulties that might arise from his election.

Adams's heavy workload soon took a toll on his health. In February 1771 Adams fell ill with chest pains. He believed at times that death was imminent, and he remained too sick to work for two months, but he gradually recovered. Historians now speculate that Adams was suffering from exhaustion and stress.

Shortly after his recovery, in April 1771, Adams moved his family back to the farm in Braintree, but he kept his office in Boston. He enjoyed having his wife and children near, but they were sometimes a distraction from his work. After the move, Adams noted in his diary that he sometimes began work at 6:00 in the morning and remained until 9:00 at night. Most nights he rode home to Braintree, but he sometimes slept at his office.

John Adams joined the Massachusetts legislature in 1770.

Adams's term in the legislature ended in 1771, and he chose not to seek reelection. He decided instead to spend time with his family and pursue his legal career. In his diary, he wrote, "Farewell Politicks."

Return to Boston

Despite leaving the legislature, John Adams still found himself spending too much time away from home. In his day, trials were not held at a centralized courthouse—instead, judges traveled from town to town in order to hear local cases. Lawyers traveled

41

Samuel Adams

★ ★ ★ ★ ★

The upheaval caused by the Stamp Act provoked another member of the Adams family to become involved in the politics of the day. Samuel Adams, a famous patriot, was John Adams's cousin. Both men became famous for their roles in the American Revolution, but their lifestyles, philosophies, and activities were vastly different.

Samuel Adams, thirteen years older than his cousin, grew up in a life of privilege. His father was a wealthy estate owner in Boston. Adams attended Harvard College and earned a master's degree in addition to his basic degree. After Samuel acquired a position as a clerk in a merchant house, his father loaned him money to start a business, but the younger Adams lost the entire sum. Samuel Adams and his father then started a brewery, but the business never prospered. He continued with the business even after the death of his father and barely earned enough to support his family.

Adams then took a job as a tax collector for the city of Boston, and as a result, became acquainted with many citizens. He joined several political clubs and was elected to the Massachusetts

the same circuit made by the judges so they could find clients to represent. Adams had participated in this judicial circuit since being admitted to the bar legislature in 1765. That same year, he participated in public protests of the Stamp Act. Adams also formed a group called the Sons of Liberty with the goal of protesting the British government. In 1773 he took part in the Boston Tea Party.

The contrasts between Samuel Adams and John Adams are striking. Samuel Adams chose to rally colonists toward independence through loud, raucous protests in the streets of Boston, whereas John Adams, known as a conservative, scholarly man and one of the best thinkers in Massachusetts, published careful but inspired essays about the steps that Americans should take to preserve their rights. Both were elected to the First and Second Continental Congresses, and both signed the Declaration of Independence.

Samuel Adams remained in Congress until 1781, then returned to Boston to continue his political work in Massachusetts. He served as governor of the Commonwealth of Massachusetts from 1793 to 1797.

Although different in so many ways, city-born Samuel Adams and farm-dweller John Adams referred to each other as brothers during their days in the Continental Congress. They enjoyed leisure activities together, which included John Adams teaching his older cousin to ride a horse, and supported each other in difficult times. Both men are remembered for their remarkable service to their country.

in 1759. Reaching some towns meant a full day's ride on horseback in every kind of weather, and Adams grew weary of the continuous travel.

Thus, in November 1772, Adams decided to move his family back to Boston. He purchased a brick house on Queen Street, not far from his office. In his diary he again vowed to avoid politics altogether. This move to Boston included the newest member of the Adams family, Thomas Boylston Adams, who was born September 15, 1772.

The Boston Tea Party

The calm that John Adams enjoyed after his departure from the legislature was broken late in 1773. New tensions surfaced when the British government decided to continue to collect taxes on tea. It further decided that only tea from designated British merchants could be sold legally in the colonies. Tea from any other country or any other merchant was declared illegal. Because most colonists of British ancestry drank huge quantities of tea, this law outraged many people. It meant that the only tea that they could legally purchase was tea that carried the tea tax; in addition, the designated tea merchants could charge virtually any price they wished, since colonists could not buy their tea elsewhere.

★

In 1773 General Charles Cornwallis was the vice treasurer of Ireland and was stationed in the Irish city of Cork.

★

As a protest, the next shipments of tea that arrived by ship in New York and Philadelphia were turned away by colonists and sent back to England. In Charleston, sales agents of the tea merchants, who feared attacks by colonists, refused to take delivery of the tea, and the tea was stored in warehouses.

Angry at the British taxation of tea, protesters dumped a shipload of tea into Boston Harbor in what became known as the Boston Tea Party.

This meant that Britain could not profit from the tax on the tea or the sale of the tea itself.

Protesters in Boston, however, took more dramatic actions. On the cold night of December 16, a group of men dressed as Native Americans boarded the *Dartmouth*, a ship loaded with tea that was anchored in Boston Harbor. Once aboard, the men broke open chests of tea and dumped them into the harbor.

Although John Adams did not take part in the Boston Tea Party, as the event was eventually called, he was excited about this protest. Adams felt that the colonists had no choice but to stand up for their rights and send a strong message to England. The Boston Tea Party proved that colonists had no intention of quietly accepting every law that Parliament passed. Furthermore, the protests in Boston, Charleston, New York, and Philadelphia served to unite the colonies in a common protest. The spirit of revolution continued to grow.

Chapter 3

THE PURSUIT OF FREEDOM

After the tea was destroyed in December 1773, Bostonians nervously awaited word from England, certain that the king would impose sanctions as punishment for their actions. When the news from England arrived in May 1774, John Adams was in the process of moving his wife and children back to their farm in Braintree.

OPPOSITE: George Washington (astride horse) took command of the Continental Army when it was formed in 1775. Adams greatly admired Washington's military and political skill.

The destruction of the tea made King George III furious. As punishment, Parliament ordered Boston Harbor closed immediately. It was to remain closed until Massachusetts paid for the ruined tea. This meant that needed goods could not enter Boston, and items for sale could not leave the city. Bostonians were not even allowed to fish in the harbor. Some colonists felt that the citizens of Massachusetts should pay for the tea, but others felt that Parliament's harsh response was an even greater reason to fight for independence. Boston's plight was on the minds of many people, even in other colonies, but especially among a number of men who were preparing to meet to discuss Britain's treatment of the colonies.

The First Continental Congress

In June 1774 plans were underway for a gathering of delegates from each of the American colonies. In Philadelphia the delegates were to discuss the American problems with England and decide upon a course of action. The meeting eventually became known as the First Continental Congress. Every colony except Georgia sent representatives to the gathering. John Adams was chosen as a delegate from Massachusetts, along with Samuel Adams, Robert Paine, and Thomas Cushing.

On September 5, 1774, the Congress convened at Carpenter's Hall for the first time. One of the first transactions was an agreement among all the colonies regarding the order to close Boston

Harbor. The delegates decided to boycott British goods throughout the colonies and to refuse to sell American goods to Britain.

At the same time, a committee of twenty-four men, including John Adams, labored to draft a Declaration of Rights and Grievances. This document would identify the rights to which Americans

The Continental Congress met for the first time at Carpenter's Hall in Philadelphia on September 5, 1774.

felt entitled, based on their status as British subjects. The paper also contained a list of actions taken by Parliament that the delegates found objectionable, such as unfair taxes, the closing of Boston Harbor, and the political power granted to British Loyalists by the king or Parliament.

The weeks that Adams spent in Philadelphia were continuously busy. Congress met five or six hours each day, including Saturdays. The committee to which Adams was appointed worked additional hours, and special sessions were sometimes called in the evenings. Delegates were regularly invited to

49

lavish dinners where more politics took place. Adams, a man never known to be idle, also made time for long walks and some sightseeing. In a letter to his wife, he wrote, "My Time is totally filled from the Moment I get out of Bed [with] Visits, Ceremonies, Company, Business, News Papers, Pamphlets."

Inspiration for Americans

Aside from designing the Declaration of Rights and Grievances and the colonial boycotts, the meeting of the Continental Congress served another valuable purpose. It gave the delegates from all over the American colonies the chance to meet each other and learn that they were alike at heart— an important lesson since the colonies were practically considered different countries. Although countless heated discussions took place in the Congress, and not everyone felt that the declaration was to their liking (some wanted to be less harsh with England while others wished to be more radical), the work of the Congress gave Americans a new sense of unity.

The Continental Congress adjourned on October 26, 1774, and John Adams and his comrades set off toward Boston on October 29, the day before Adams's thirty-ninth birthday. The men were pleased with the work they had done; the colonies agreed to support each other and to preserve the rights of Americans rather than give in to the pressures instituted by England.

When word of the Congress's decisions spread through the colonies, the newspapers were flooded with letters and essays written by outspoken colonists. Some felt the Congress had not done enough, while others believed the delegates had marched the Americans straight into a war. Adams, never one to miss an opportunity to place his opinions before the public eye, wrote a series of twelve essays during this time. He signed these letters to the newspapers "Novanglus," a word that meant "New Englander."

In his articles Adams made two major points. The first was that the future of America was in danger due to a conspiracy among members of the corrupt British government who wished to plunder the riches of the colonies. His second issue was that all groups of people had the right and the ability to govern themselves. The articles were well written and full of theories and citations from famous philosophers, but they were rather long and difficult for the average colonist to read. These anonymous letters were among many newspaper articles written by outraged colonists, and such writings eventually caught the attention of King George and Parliament.

The Battles of Lexington and Concord

In response to the documents created by the Congress and the calls for action in the newspapers, British officials decided to stifle the rebellion that seemed sure to come. On April 19, 1775, red-coated British soldiers marched westward from Boston to

51

This engraving depicts the Battle of Lexington where, on April 19, 1775, British soldiers and American militiamen exchanged the first fire of the Revolutionary War.

Lexington on their way to Concord, where the colonists had stored a large quantity of gunpowder and weapons. The British commanders foresaw an easy victory—the Americans were poorly prepared, they thought, and would be taken by surprise.

Instead, the eight hundred British soldiers met resistance at Lexington and faced a well-prepared American militia at Concord. The redcoats, as the British troops were called, damaged only a small portion of the munitions and were turned back to Boston after they lost many men. The colonists themselves lost nearly one hundred lives.

John Adams was preparing to return to Philadelphia for the Second Continental Congress when he received word of this unprovoked and bloody event. He rode out to Concord and Lexington to see the sites for himself and listen to eyewitness reports of the incident. About one week later, he departed for Philadelphia.

The Second Continental Congress

Congress convened on May 10, 1775, with John Adams, Samuel Adams, Robert Paine, and John Hancock representing Massachusetts. The delegates met in the Pennsylvania State House, and this time, Georgia sent a representative to the Congress, meaning that all thirteen colonies were represented.

Before the month was over, the delegates decided to issue the first Continental money. It needed money to finance the rebellion against England, and it needed a uniform currency that could be used throughout the colonies.

The attacks upon Lexington and Concord meant that Great Britain had declared war on Massachusetts. Other colonies raised armies for their own defense, but none considered themselves to be at war. With Massachusetts targeted by Britain, the Congress needed to make swift decisions to assist the colony. After weeks of debates, the delegates voted to create a Continental army that would be staffed and paid for by all the colonies. The Continental army could then be sent to defend any colony against the Britain.

★
Many British subjects refused to volunteer to fight in the American Revolution because the Americans fought so fiercely.
★

53

The Dangers of Congress

★ ★ ★ ★ ★

While war raged in the colonies, the delegates of the Continental Congresses met in Carpenter's Hall and the Pennsylvania State House in Philadelphia, which was considered one of the most beautiful cities in the New World. Although the delegates were far from the battlefields, they were not insulated from the perils of war. In fact, they were in grave danger.

As far as British officials were concerned, the delegates were guilty of treason—the crime of attempting to overthrow the government. Had they been captured and found guilty of treason, their punishment would have been death by hanging. In July 1777,

Congress then debated the selection of a commander for the entire Continental army. After less than two days of discussion, the position was given to George Washington, whom John Adams greatly admired. Washington was a wealthy plantation owner who commanded Virginia's small army for five years during the French and Indian War and performed many acts of valor. He was active in organizing boycotts and protests in when British soldiers descended on Philadelphia, the delegates fled to safety. The British did not capture a single member of Congress.

The men in Congress also worried about their families and property. John Adams experienced a particularly anxious time when the British army fought in and around Boston. He worried about his wife and children, his farm, and characteristically, his books. He advised his wife to flee into the wooded hills behind the farm if the family was in danger. His anxiety about not being at home to defend his family was extreme.

Signing the Declaration of Independence also meant trouble. For the delegates, signing this document was as good as admitting that they were criminals. In the days when Britain thought that it would regain control of its colonies, the government created a list of war criminals and determined what their fates would be if they were captured. Some would be pardoned and set free— others would not. John Adams learned later in his life that if he had been convicted of the crimes listed against him, he would have been hanged.

Virginia against Britain's unfair laws. On June 23, 1775, George Washington departed Philadelphia to assume command of the army.

Adams quickly became a respected leader among the delegates. His experience at the First Continental Congress had given him confidence in the meetings. At this gathering, his fellow delegates began to recognize his great intellect and his ability to solve problems. Adams also became known for his capacity for hard work. He served on ninety committees, more than any other delegate, and was the chairperson of twenty-four of his committees.

Following the formation of the army, the congress discussed weapons and supplies for the army, whether to reconcile or break with England, and matters of trade with England and other countries. In late July 1775, Congress adjourned for a three-week break. Adams and his fellow delegates hurried home to Massachusetts, but Adams saw little of his family. Instead, he visited George Washington's army encampment as well as the Massachusetts legislature to discuss political matters with its representatives.

The Second Continental Congress reconvened in September 1775. The most immediate concern was the reinforcement of the army. Washington needed food, supplies, gunpowder, and more men, and he faced a number of organizational problems as the leader of a new army. Congress acted quickly to gather and send supplies to Washington and to resolve issues such as payments, rank, and promotions for the men.

Two important events took place in November 1775. During the First Continental Congress, a petition had been drafted and sent to King George asking for reconciliation between the colonies and the king. Adams was in the minority of delegates who had opposed this petition. He thought that the king would only treat the colonies like rebellious children and impose more laws. Nearly a year later, the Congress learned that King George had rejected the petition and declared the colonies to be in a full state of rebellion. Everyone realized that the war would soon escalate.

At the same time, Congress worked to create a navy. It acquired a small number of ships, placed orders for more ships, hired marines, and arranged for supplies. John Adams was a member of the Naval Committee, and after extensive research into the construction of ships and weapons, he helped draft rules concerning ships, sailors, provisions, and conduct. Because he felt that the war against Britain could not be won without a navy, Adams found his work on this committee to be a great source of pride and satisfaction.

Further Concerns of Congress

Several colonies soon approached the Continental Congress for advice. They wished to know how to govern themselves. In many cases,—officials who had been appointed by Parliament or the king had already been removed from office. According to the English charters that had first established them, the colonies were still ruled by England. The Continental Congress advised each colony to design and create its own government that would be independent of England.

While the delegates struggled with the future of the colonies, they also worried about the effects of the war on their homes. British troops caused great damage in Maine, Massachusetts, and Virginia. The Americans asked for help from France and

In January 1776, Thomas Paine (above) published *Common Sense* (below), a pamphlet that promoted the idea of independence in the colonies.

COMMON SENSE;

ADDRESSED TO THE

INHABITANTS

OF

AMERICA,

On the following interesting

SUBJECTS.

I. Of the Origin and Defign of Government in general, with concife Remarks on the Englifh Conftitution.

II. Of Monarchy and Hereditary Succeffion.

III. Thoughts on the prefent State of American Affairs.

IV. Of the prefent Ability of America, with fome mifcellaneous Reflections.

A NEW EDITION, with feveral Additions in the Body of the Work. To which is added an APPENDIX ; together with an Addrefs to the People called QUAKERS.

N. B. The New Addition here given increafes the Work upwards of one Third.

Man knows no Mafter fave creating HEAVEN, Or thofe whom Choice and common Good ordain.
THOMSON.

Spain but received none. These countries still regarded the colonies as the property of England; France and Spain knew that aiding the colonies would surely put themselves at war with England. The colonists began to realize that the only way to receive help from France or Spain would be to break free of England.

In January 1776 a small pamphlet called *Common Sense* was published in New York by a man named Thomas Paine. In it, Paine spoke out against the rule of kings and promoted the idea of independence. The pamphlet was widely read and helped to turn popular opinion toward separating the colonies from Britain. Adams purchased two copies and sent one home to his wife. Although he was delighted that the pamphlet was swaying people toward the idea of independence,

John Adams

Adams felt that Paine's understanding of government was poor and that his reasoning was weak.

John Adams and many others in the Continental Congress had favored independence for some time, but they knew they had to wait until the time was right. If a vote for independence failed, it might mean a split between the colonies that sought independence and those that favored reconciliation with England. If some of the colonies reconciled, they might eventually conquer those that voted for independence.

★

In the summer of 1776 demand for *Common Sense* grew faster than copies could be printed.

★

Adams and his colleagues waited patiently. They knew that the popularity of *Common Sense* was turning more colonists in favor of independence. They also knew that if the colonists hoped to receive aid from France or Spain, separation from England was crucial. The chance of foreign military aid might turn even more colonists in favor of a break from England.

Independence drew closer when the delegates received disturbing news. The British government was sending thousands of German mercenary soldiers, known as Hessians, to fight against the colonists. Even the delegates who hoped to reconcile with England could see that the king was not about to give up. Hiring these soldiers meant that the king did not intend to compromise—he planned to win. The possibility of reconciliation with England was gone. If the colonists did not wish to be conquered, their only option was to win their independence.

Movement Toward Independence

In May 1776 John Adams still feared that a vote for independence would fail. Instead of trying to lobby delegates for their votes, Adams found a different way to push for independence. On May 10, he introduced a resolution for each colony to reorganize its government to exclude all aspects of their English origin. This meant redesigning jobs, removing officials who were agents of the king, and installing representatives who earned the support of their people. By tearing down its old government and building anew, each colony thus became a free and independent state. When the resolution was easily passed on May 15, John Adams was thrilled. Independence was nearly accomplished.

The final step toward freedom began on June 7, 1776. Richard Henry Lee of Virginia placed a motion before the Congress. It contained three objectives: that the independent states be declared free of Britain; that the states build alliances with foreign countries; and that the states unite to form a confederation. John Adams seconded the motion, and the debates began.

The first two days of debates were heated and bitter. Some delegates declared that the colonists did not yet wish for separation from England; others argued that the colonists were simply waiting for Congress to lead them to independence. Nothing was accomplished. Congress postponed the discussion until July 1 to allow delegates to receive instructions from home.

In the meantime, a committee was appointed to draw up a declaration of independence. Delegates who wished to break with England wanted a document ready so no time would be wasted if Lee's motion was approved. Assigned to the committee were Benjamin Franklin, Robert Livingston, Roger Sherman, Thomas Jefferson, and John Adams. The committee discussed the important topics for the document, then asked Adams and Jefferson to prepare the declaration.

Thomas Jefferson was a thirty-three-year-old delegate from Virginia. He was a respected lawyer, plantation owner, and member of government in his home province. He did not attend the First Continental Congress, and he rarely spoke out

A nineteenth-century painting shows Adams (center) as he works closely with Thomas Jefferson (right) and Benjamin Franklin (left) to draft the Declaration of Independence.

61

during the Second Congress. Jefferson was polite, diplomatic, and well educated, and was recognized for his excellent work in drafting several documents for the government in Virginia. He worked closely with John Adams on a few committees, and their relationship was friendly.

The two men agreed upon the details of the document, then discussed which of them should write the final draft. Adams, who was serving on twenty-three committees, carried a tremendous workload. In his autobiography, he later recalled his personal opinion that Jefferson was better suited for the job. Jefferson agreed to the task and then returned to his lodgings to write the declaration.

Jefferson showed the document first to Adams, then to the rest of the committee. A few changes were made, then the declaration was presented to the entire Continental Congress on July 1, 1776. The prospect of independence still teetered uncertainly until the Congress could debate and vote.

John Adams's rival throughout the Continental Congresses was Pennsylvanian John Dickinson, who favored reconciliation with England. When the debate over independence began, Dickinson arose and spoke at length against the disaster that would befall the colonies if they separated from Britain. He was convinced that the colonies would lose the war and that afterward Britain would hold even greater control over them.

When Dickinson finished, the room fell silent for a time, then John Adams arose. Without notes or a script, he spoke for two hours, describing a bright, independent future for the colonies. Many delegates spoke that day, but Adams made a lasting impression upon many. In a letter, Richard Stockton of New Jersey wrote to his son, "The man to whom the country is most indebted for the great measure of independency is Mr. John Adams of Boston. I call him the Atlas of American Independence." The Atlas to whom he referred was the character in Greek mythology who carried the world on his shoulders.

The Vote for Independence

According to the custom of the Congress, a preliminary vote was taken that day. Nine of the thirteen colonies, a clear majority, voted in favor of separating from Britain, but it was not enough. The delegates realized that unless they showed King George that they were completely united in their desire for independence, the king would try to pit the colonies against each other. The delegates knew that their plans for independence required a unanimous vote to split from Britain. The official vote would take place the next day, on July 2, 1776.

The evening of July 1 was a busy one for the Philadelphia delegates. Some reconsidered their choices; some received new orders for the vote from their home colonies; a rider was sent to summon one delegate who was ill at home.

The vote was quickly taken on July 2. Twelve of the thirteen colonies voted for independence; New

To the delight of Adams and his colleagues, twelve of the thirteen colonies voted for independence on July 2, 1776, at the Second Continental Congress (pictured).

York abstained from voting rather than vote in opposition. The colonies were now politically separate from England. John Adams and his fellows were jubilant. July 2, 1776, had become the day of independence for the American colonies.

On July 3 and 4, Congress considered the declaration that Jefferson had drafted. A number of changes were made to the document. Around the middle of the day on July 4, the Declaration of Independence was approved by twelve colonies, with New York again abstaining from the vote. Congressional president John Hancock and secretary Charles Thomson signed the document. About a month later, the rest of the delegates signed a formal version of the declaration.

In a letter to his wife following the vote for independence, Adams revealed his emotions about the importance of the event:

The Second Day of July 1776, will be the most memorable Epochs, in the History of America. . . . It ought to be commemorated, as the Day of Deliverance by solemn Acts of

Devotion to God Almighty. It ought to be solemnized with Pomp and Parade, with Shews, Games, Sports, Guns, Bells, Bonfires and Illuminations from one End of this Continent to the other from this Time forward forever more.

Despite his pleasure at the accomplishments of Congress, Adams admitted to his wife that difficult years still lay ahead. The war would intensify before peace could be achieved. Lives would be lost and property would be damaged. The Americans would have to undergo tough times if they were to secure the freedom they now tasted.

Adams also felt that the Congress's most difficult work lay ahead. The colonies were completely free of English rule, but a new government was needed to protect the rights and freedoms of Americans. The immensity of this task was not lost on Adams. In an essay titled "Thoughts on Government," he wrote that he and his colleagues in Congress "have been sent into life at a time when the greatest lawgivers of antiquity would have wished to live. How few of the human race have ever enjoyed an opportunity of making an election of government." Adams went on to explain that at no time in history had human beings had any more control over their government than they had control of the weather. The Continental Congress faced the unique—and intimidating—opportunity of building a government completely from scratch.

Chapter 4

STRUGGLES OF A NEW NATION

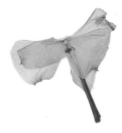

Having announced the colonies' independence, Congress faced enormous tasks. First, every colony needed to design and ratify its own constitution to create an official state government. Congress then needed to draft articles of confederation to unite the states as a country. A government for the new country had to be designed and ratified in order to pursue the business of the nation. To complicate matters, all of this work had to be accomplished while fighting the war with Britain.

OPPOSITE: After British forces defeated his army in the Battle of Long Island, George Washington evacuated all of his troops from the island under cover of night.

To add to the difficulty, many of the delegates suffered from illnesses brought on by exhaustion, stress, and the pain of separation from their families. By the time the Declaration of Independence was approved, John Adams had not seen his wife or children in six months. A number of delegates were forced to leave Congress for several weeks or months in order to regain their health.

John Adams remained a member of numerous committees, which meant many additional hours of work outside the daily meetings of Congress. The most demanding and stressful of these was the Board of War. While Washington commanded the troops and took charge of military matters, Adams and four other men handled the business of the war—everything from food, supplies, and gunpowder to recruitment, discipline, and promotions. These five men shouldered the huge responsibility of directing funds to feed and clothe the army, ensuring that weapons and supplies were sent where they were needed, and seeking aid from foreign countries to assist the war effort.

The Battle of Long Island

During the uneasy summer of 1776, Adams, the Board of War, and the entire Congress knew that in addition to the many British soldiers already stationed throughout the countryside, thousands of British and German troops and hundreds of ships had arrived at New York in July 1776. On August 27, the British and Germans began an attack on

Long Island. The Americans quickly lost hundreds of men and were at risk of losing the entire army.

The battle paused temporarily, then a heavy fog rolled in. After nightfall, Washington succeeded in evacuating the whole army off the island and across the East River, through rain and fog in every imaginable type of boat. When dawn broke and the fog faded, the British commanders were startled to see that every American was gone.

Congress praised Washington for his resourcefulness. The Battle of Long Island had been lost, and the British controlled New York City, but the entire war might have been lost if not for the general's actions. Following a number of poor showings by the Continental army and a huge number of desertions, Washington wrote to Congress begging for more men as well as better pay and training for soldiers. Adams and the Board of War increased the soldiers' pay, offered land to some, and tried to improve conditions for the men. It also created tougher regulations and penalties for deserters.

★

In October 1776 British forces defeated George Washington's army in the Battle of White Plains.

★

Hardships at Home

The Board of War placed constant demands on John Adams, but in October 1776, after nearly nine months of uninterrupted service to Congress, he was granted a leave to return home. He remained in Braintree for nine weeks before once again departing for Congress in January 1777. This was an especially difficult farewell, for Abigail Adams

69

Abigail Adams

While John Adams traveled to Boston and beyond to fulfill the duties of his law career, his young wife, Abigail, remained at home to oversee the business of the farm. This task was complicated by the fact that women had few rights in the 1700s; they could not vote or purchase property, for example. Nevertheless, Abigail Adams successfully managed the household and farm while looking after her five children.

Throughout all of her husband's adventures, Abigail Adams remained a source of strength to her family. In her letters, she vowed not to complain to her husband about her hardships at home. While the Continental Congresses took place, John Adams was gone for up to nine months at a time, but Abigail Adams managed the farm so well that her husband once wrote that he doubted if he could have done better.

John Adams depended on his wife not only as a caretaker for their children and farm, but also for her intelligence and advice. In the midst of the chaos of the Revolution, Abigail Adams was a steadying influence on whom he could rely. While in Philadelphia, Adams valued her letters for her reports of the war and conditions at home. She was introduced to George Washington and several other generals, and was invited to dinners with them a number of times. She carefully recorded the details of these important meetings and passed them along to her husband.

John and Abigail Adams's letters to each other reveal the high regard that they held for each other. John Adams wrote to his wife as an equal, and revealed his concerns and problems. In an era when women were expected to obey their husbands unconditionally, Abigail Adams felt completely comfortable in expressing her thoughts to her spouse. During the Second Continental Congress, she wrote to him:

> In the new Code of Laws which I suppose it will be necessary for you to make I desire you would Remember the Ladies, and be more generous and favourable to them than your ancestors. Do not put such unlimited power into the hands of the Husbands. Remember all Men would be tyrants if they could. If perticuliar care and attention is not paid to the Ladies we are determined to foment a Rebelion, and will not hold ourselves bound by any Laws in which we have no voice, or Representation.

Her words were not mean-spirited or threatening, but written as a good-natured tease to her husband. In his reply, John Adams joked that men were already ruled by "the petticoat."

Abigail Adams is remembered for her strength, spirit, and intelligence in an age when women lived sheltered lives. She is also remembered as a true patriot who was willing to sacrifice her own comfort to allow her husband to continue his important work. John Adams's pride and admiration for his wife is evident in a letter he sent her from the Continental Congress: "It gives me more Pleasure than I can express to learn that you sustain with so much Fortitude, the Shocks and Terrors of the Times. You are really brave, my dear, you are an Heroine."

was pregnant again. Yet the Board of War, the Articles of Confederation, and Adams's twenty-six committees beckoned. In July, John Adams was unable to get away from Congress to be with his wife when their baby daughter was stillborn.

Across the colonies, battles and territory were won and lost, but Adams, the chairman of the Board of War, remained optimistic in 1777. A key confrontation began in July, when British troops in New York crammed into ships and sailed along the Delaware River for Philadelphia. In September, the British troops attacked and gained control of Philadelphia, but the American army remained whole. Adams felt strongly that since the American army had survived for two years, it could continue to endure and eventually win the war. The attack on Philadelphia had not, as the British hoped, broken up the Continental Congress. Delegates had regrouped in York, Pennsylvania.

Unity for the Colonies

Between June and November of 1777, a committee of thirteen delegates, one from each colony, had drafted, reviewed, and finalized the Articles of Confederation. This document would officially unite the thirteen colonies as a new nation. On November 17, 1777, Congress voted to accept the Articles of Confederation, creating the United States of America.

Because of the daily demands of the Board of War and his other committees, John Adams had avoided becoming involved in this important endeavor. In fact, Adams had departed for home six days before the vote. His writings reveal that he intended to decline any further term in Congress and stay home for good.

John Adams's service to his country, however, was far from finished. At the end of November, after only fifteen days at home, he learned that Congress wished to send him as an emissary to France. There, he was to assist American diplomats in obtaining weapons and other aid for the war and to negotiate trade and a possible alliance.

Adams had heard hints of this assignment before leaving Philadelphia, but Abigail Adams was stunned by the news. She feared that she might never see her husband again—ocean voyages were always dangerous, even more so in wartime. Yet she knew that her husband, who was deeply concerned about the affairs of his country and felt honored by this appointment, would not turn down the assignment.

A Journey to France

On February 15, 1778, John Adams set sail for France aboard a ship called *Boston*. His companion was his ten-year-old son, John Quincy. Six weeks later, the ship docked at Bordeaux, and the two made their way to Paris. The colonies had already received aid from France in the form of firearms, gunpowder, and uniforms, but Adams hoped to gain more military aid and possibly a treaty of support.

While Adams lived in France as an emissary for the colonies from late 1777 to early 1779, he helped obtain military aid and reviewed French troops (pictured).

Adams immediately met with Benjamin Franklin, who was already negotiating in Paris. John Adams quickly learned that about ten days before his departure from Massachusetts, Franklin had signed a treaty with France. This agreement established conditions for commerce and procured the assistance of French soldiers plus other military aid. Adams feared that his long journey had been a waste of time. Determined to make the best of it, he stayed in France to assist Franklin and Arthur Lee, the other member of the American commission. He set their neglected bookkeeping in order, tried to learn French, read magazines and newspapers from London, and wrote reports to Congress.

Adams enjoyed Paris and the French people, and he was introduced to King Louis XVI and the queen, Marie-Antoinette, in May 1778. The formal dinner with the king and queen impressed John Adams greatly. His time in France was not easy, however; he did not speak French well, he missed his family, and news from home or from Congress was painfully slow—letters often took months to cross the ocean.

The Voyage Home

Although Adams might have lingered in France while he awaited orders from Congress, he hated to be idle. Since Franklin's treaty with France settled many trade issues and procured troops and military aid, Adams wrote to Congress to advise that Benjamin Franklin was the only American needed in Paris. In February 1779 word arrived that Franklin should remain in Paris; Lee was to move to Madrid, Spain; and Adams could return home. Adams and his son sailed for home and arrived in Boston on August 2. They had been gone nearly eighteen months.

In Paris news of the war had been scarce, and Adams was glad to be home to assess the situation firsthand. Washington's army had trained a great deal over the past winter and had been more successful against British forces, but the war had not yet turned in favor of either side.

In September 1779, the *Bonhomme Richard*, under Captain John Paul Jones, defeated the British ship *Serapis* in the largest naval battle of the Revolution.

The Massachusetts Constitution

Adams was home for only a week when Braintree elected him as a representative to the Massachusetts constitutional convention. On September 1, 1779, he departed for Cambridge, only ten miles from home. He was elected to the committee to draft the constitution for Massachusetts, and then was chosen to write the document for the approval of all.

John Adams faced an opportunity unlike any other. With a deep knowledge of philosophy, government,

75

and the law acquired from his years of reading, coupled with an enjoyment of writing, he was ideally suited to draft one of Massachusetts's most important documents. Having read other state constitutions and using his essay "Thoughts on Government" as a guide, he completed the draft in about one month and delivered it to the committee for review by the end of October 1779, very near his forty-fourth birthday.

After making only minor changes, Adams's committee recommended his draft to the constitutional convention. The representatives made a few further changes. To Adams's great delight, a section outlining the commonwealth's duty to educate its citizens passed "unanimously without amendment." He had feared that this passage, the first of its kind in any state constitution, would be stricken.

Following the delegates' approval, the document was published and distributed for a popular vote. The constitution of the Commonwealth of Massachusetts was then approved on October 25, 1780.

The Journey Toward Peace

Before Adams had even finished his draft of the Massachusetts constitution, a new assignment arrived from Philadelphia. Congress had voted unanimously to send John Adams back to France to negotiate peace whenever Britain was ready to discuss terms. With the war nowhere near a conclusion, this assignment could keep Adams in France for many years. He did not hesitate to accept, however, because he realized the monumental importance of being selected to negotiate peace with Britain.

In November 1779 John Adams set sail aboard the ship *La Sensible*. John Quincy, now twelve years old, and Charles,

Adams became frustrated with French officials (pictured), who were slow to provide the support he requested.

nearly ten, were his companions for the three-thousand-mile voyage. Abigail Adams, daughter Nabby, who was fourteen, and son Thomas, only seven, remained at home. The Adamses reached Paris on February 9, 1780. Adams enrolled his sons in an academy the very next day and made arrangements to visit with the foreign minister of France.

Adams had several matters in mind as he prepared to visit with French officials. First, he knew that many Americans were suffering food shortages and financial difficulties as a result of the war. Second, the war was virtually at a stalemate—neither side was on the brink of victory. Third, Adams felt strongly that the French navy might turn the war in favor of the Americans.

As a diplomat, Adams knew that issues of such importance had to be approached slowly. On his first visit with the French foreign minister, he learned that France was already dispatching ships and more troops to engage in the war against

77

Britain. For the next several months, however, Adams struggled in a quagmire of France's political posturing. France's agent wanted Adams to do nothing, because he feared that the Britain might expect America and France to surrender together if the Americans lost. Adams discovered that France did not regard the colonies as an equal partner but as a weak dependent. He worried that France did not care about the future of the Americans or their independence, but only about its chance to damage England, its old enemy.

With little actual work to be done, Adams began to write. He produced articles anonymously for French newspapers and under a pseudonym for British papers. These were designed to educate British and French citizens to the plight of Americans and attempt to gain favor for the American cause. Although this activity kept Adams busy, he was anxious for a task of real importance.

An Appeal to the Netherlands

Adams knew that Congress planned to appeal to the Netherlands (or Holland) for aid. Frustrated by matters in France and eager to gain financial help for his country, he set out for Amsterdam accompanied by his sons on July 27, 1780, without waiting for approval from Congress.

On August 10, John Adams and his children arrived in Amsterdam, the busiest port in Europe. In September, he received the consent of Congress to seek loans from the Netherlands, but he faced

78

an extremely difficult task. The Dutch people understood little of the situation in America. They would never consent to a loan if the colonies seemed likely to fall back into the hands of England. The Dutch government did not recognize the United States as a country and therefore would not listen to an American representative. In addition, the colonial army lost a number of important battles in 1780, leaving the prospect of winning the war in doubt. The winter of 1780 was a gloomy one in every respect for John Adams.

Not until May 1781 was Adams granted a meeting with government officials in The Hague. The meeting was futile—Adams gained neither recognition of the United States nor any loans. As in France, Adams found himself once again frustrated by a political limbo. To keep busy, he published articles in the Dutch newspapers to garner public support for Americans and sent numerous reports home to Congress.

★

In the summer of 1780 the University of Pennsylvania awarded an honorary Master of Arts degree to Thomas Paine for his writing.

★

Separation and Sickness

In July 1781 an unprecedented opportunity arose for fourteen-year-old John Quincy. Francis Dana, an aide to Adams, was instructed by Congress to visit Saint Petersburg, Russia, to seek official recognition of the United States from Empress Catherine the Great. Because the court language of Russia was French, Dana asked John Quincy, who spoke fluent French, to accompany him as secretary and interpreter. Both Adams and his son saw the opportunity that the trip afforded, and John Quincy left with Dana.

At the same time, Adams decided to send his son Charles home to Massachusetts. The boy had suffered bouts of illness and missed his mother terribly. On August 12, Charles boarded the ship *South Carolina* with a family friend and reached home safely.

Days after Charles's departure, John Adams became terribly ill. Others in the house suffered the same symptoms, which included fever, delirium, and weakness. The sickness lasted several weeks. In October, Adams slowly regained his health, but he struggled with depression over his lack of success in Holland and the outlook for the war at home. He did not learn until the end of November that on October 19, 1781, the British army, led by General Charles Cornwallis, had surrendered to the combined American and French forces at Yorktown, Virginia. The war had turned, and the Americans were at last victorious.

This engraving shows the surrender of British general Charles Cornwallis at Yorktown, Virginia, on October 19, 1781.

Freedom Within Reach

Despite the momentous victory, John Adams knew that the war was not completely over. Many British troops remained in America, which meant confrontations would still erupt. A peace agreement had to be reached. And still, the Americans needed money to support the army until the last British soldier sailed for home.

Although still weak from his illness, Adams renewed his efforts to be recognized by the Netherlands and to acquire loans. In mid-April of 1782, he was officially recognized by the government of Holland as the ambassador from the United States. The home and offices that Adams established in the Netherlands became the first American embassy in the world.

In June, Adams's persistence resulted in a loan of $2 million from several Dutch banks, money that Congress badly needed. Adams took great pride in this accomplishment and felt that it made his time in Holland worthwhile. In September 1782 he signed a treaty of commerce with the Netherlands.

Negotiation of Peace

Shortly after signing the treaty, Adams received a summons from John Jay, a member of the American peace commission, who was making preparations for peace negotiations in Paris. Adams departed for Paris to join Jay and Benjamin Franklin.

John Jay had begun preliminary negotiations with England's Richard Oswald over the summer, but Jay informed Oswald that formal negotiations would not begin until Britain acknowledged the independence of the United States. In late September, after many communications with British officials, Oswald received approval to recognize the United States of America. This was an important political and moral victory.

Jay had made a bold move. Upon his appointment to the peace commission, he had been instructed by Congress to follow the lead of the French in all matters. French delegates had insisted that the issue of independence be ignored, confirming Adams's earlier suspicions that France cared only about its feud with England and not about American interests. Jay, however, refused to be controlled by the French or to let recognition of American independence be cast aside. His persistence had attained Britain's formal recognition of the United States.

Benjamin Franklin (seated at desk), Adams, and John Jay negotiated peace with British representatives. In 1783 both sides signed the Treaty of Paris, which officially ended the American Revolution.

When Adams reached Paris and met with Jay, he was outraged to learn that the Americans had been instructed to abide by the wishes of the French. Adams wrote to Congress to say that he and Jay would rather quit the delegation than follow the French. Franklin also agreed that the Americans should negotiate without French directives.

The three Americans entered negotiations with representatives from England on October 30. At issue were the boundaries of the United States, rights to the Mississippi River, American fishing rights off Newfoundland, debts, and the treatment of British loyalists who remained in America. These discussions went quickly, and one of the delegates returned to London for approval of the agreements. He arrived back in Paris on November 25.

On Saturday, November 30, 1782, Adams and the rest of the commission signed the preliminary peace treaty along with representatives from England. The documents were sent to America and England for approval by the respective governments. The delegates from both countries relaxed over dinner together that evening in joyous spirits.

John Adams was far from idle while waiting for approval of the peace treaty, and he sent many communications to Congress. He visited The Hague in July, 1783, to discuss a trade matter and to reunite with John Quincy, who had returned from Russia in April. Adams and his son returned to Paris together in August 1783.

Nearly a year after the preliminary agreement was completed, the official peace documents known as the Treaty of Paris were signed on September 3, 1783. The war was over, the revolution had ended, and the United States of America was free.

Chapter 5

THE GROWING PAINS
OF GOVERNMENT

With the peace treaty signed, John Adams wondered what his next task would be. Since his first day in the Continental Congress on September 5, 1774, nine years earlier nearly to the day, he had worked ceaselessly for the good of his country. The hardest jobs—independence and a victory in the war—had been accomplished.

Adams realized that diplomacy was in his blood. Returning to his legal practice in Boston would never satisfy him. The position he desired most was that of minister to England so he could help to reconcile the United States with its former parent. In the past nine years, however, he had been home for less than fifteen months. Aware that much work remained in Europe, he begged his wife to join him. After arranging for sons Charles and Thomas to live with an uncle, Abigail Adams and nineteen-year-old Nabby sailed for London. On August 7, 1784, John Adams was reunited with his wife and daughter.

OPPOSITE: Adams, who had served his country as a lawyer, diplomat, and vice president, became the second president of the United States of America in 1797.

Minister to England

Diplomatic matters still required John Adams's presence in France, so the family set up housekeeping in a mansion in Auteuil, near Paris. Thomas Jefferson, also in Paris as a diplomat, became one of the family's closest friends.

When word arrived from Congress in April 1785 that John Adams was named minister to England, the moment was bittersweet. Adams had petitioned for this position, but he was reluctant to uproot his contented family and depart from his close friend Jefferson. Much work awaited him in England, however, so in May the Adams family departed for London. John Quincy, not quite eighteen years old, sailed for America in order to attend college at Harvard.

Adams's first meeting in London was a private audience with King George III on June 1, 1785. He was as nervous as he had been at age fifteen when he rode alone to his examinations at Harvard. Adams was the only American in a crowded room of English lords, bishops, and statesmen as he was presented to the king. His name had been known to King George for several years—as an American rebel. Adams

King George III (left) granted Adams a private audience for their first meeting. Adams began his service as minister to England in 1785.

stood face to face with the man whom so many Americans despised.

During the brief reception, Adams's voice was shaky, but the meeting went well. King George, two years younger than Adams, was polite and cordial, and he approved of Adams's presence as a diplomat. The success of the encounter was not to be typical of Adams's acceptance in England, however.

To nearly everyone in England, Americans were considered troublemakers or selfish brats who had thrown a tantrum to get their way and had won. The English people with whom John and Abigail Adams interacted were usually polite, but by no means friendly. The American couple found difficulty socializing. John Adams was unfairly criticized in the newspapers because of the English hatred of Americans, but he weathered their slander, as Jefferson noted, with remarkable ease.

Adams faced numerous obstacles. As minister to England, he tried to resolve debts between the British and the Americans, establish healthy trade relations, and hasten the withdrawal of British soldiers that remained in America. He wrote letters to British government officials to ask for cooperation in meeting the terms of the Treaty of Paris but sometimes received no reply for several months, and then the officials refused to act. He asked that American ships be allowed to deliver their goods to Canada, the West Indies, and England but was ignored. Britain would allow American goods into its empire only on British ships.

In August 1786
Congress adopted a
coinage system for the
new nation.

★

The United States was desperately poor after the war, and Britain knew it. Although Adams secured a loan from Holland in May 1786, his attempts in England to acquire loans and increase American exports to improve the economy were stonewalled by British officials. When Adams asked Britain to withdraw its soldiers from America as dictated by the Treaty of Paris, he was told that since the United States also violated the treaty by failing to pay debts, Britain refused to be pressured into keeping its part of the bargain. Adams saw that the British harbored a grudge against the United States that he could not overcome.

John Adams and his family frequently became homesick for Massachusetts. One of the happier moments of their years in London, though, was Nabby's marriage in 1786 to Colonel William Smith, an American military officer. Later, on April 2, 1787, Nabby gave birth to a baby boy, John and Abigail Adams's first grandchild.

Drafting of the Constitution

Aware that he was accomplishing very little in England and that a convention was underway in Philadelphia to design the United States government, Adams began to write a small book called *A Defence of the Constitutions of Government of the United States of America*. At a London print shop he had a number of copies printed in January 1787 and sent one to Jefferson and several more to his friends in Congress.

A painting depicts members of Congress as they sign the U.S. Constitution. The signing of the Constitution took place while Adams continued to work in England.

According to some of the delegates at the convention, Adams's booklet provided excellent principles to consider while shaping the new government. While Adams remained in England, the convention finished its draft of the Constitution on September 17, 1787, and the document was ratified on June 21, 1788. The United States had completed the final step in establishing itself as a new nation.

Return to Massachusetts

Early in 1787 John Adams had written to Congress asking to be recalled to America. In December of that year he received approval for his request. Nabby, her husband, and her son sailed for New York. John and Abigail Adams sailed for Massachusetts on March 30, 1788. John Adams had not seen his

89

farm in Braintree nor his youngest son, Thomas, in nearly nine years.

Adams had no idea what the future would hold in Massachusetts. While still in England, he had purchased a home in Braintree that he had always admired and eventually named Peacefield. As for employment, however, Adams was uncertain. He first needed to study the political climate in the United States, from which he had been removed for nine years.

The decision was easier than Adams expected. Arriving in Boston, John and Abigail Adams received a grand welcome. Church bells tolled, and the Adamses were met at their ship by messengers who escorted them to the home of Governor John Hancock for a festive welcome party. In the days that followed, John Adams was asked to consider numerous jobs, but the one he desired most was vice president of the United States.

Vice President John Adams

Nearly everyone in Congress was certain that George Washington would be elected president, but the vice presidency remained in question. In February 1789 the vote was taken. George Washington was unanimously elected president, and John Adams was elected vice president by a comfortable margin. The men were inaugurated in April in New York City, the temporary capital of the United States.

Accustomed to hard work and great activity, Adams was somewhat frustrated as vice president.

The position offered little power or responsibility. Apart from his role as president of the Senate, in which he never voted except in a tie, his duties were light. Even his business interactions with the president were rare.

One factor in Adams's lack of influence as vice president was a shift in his political thinking. He had recently published articles and spoken in favor of the government containing a layer that represented the elite of the population. Some portion of the government, he maintained, should consist of persons who had acquired a certain level of wealth, which presumably indicated that such people were more intelligent or of better judgment than the rest. The shift in his thinking was curious, and his theory alienated some people. Some historians speculate that the change resulted from his many years of living in Europe among the upper class.

In this illustration of the swearing in of George Washington as the first president of the United States, John Adams, vice president, stands behind Washington.

To some of Adams's colleagues, several of whom had been at the Continental Congress, this opinion opposed the spirit of the

Revolution. Even the newly appointed secretary of state, Thomas Jefferson, who considered Adams a close friend, found Adams's new thinking to be distasteful. Some, including Jefferson, worried that Adams wished to install a king in America, but this was untrue. Jefferson, although always polite, soon maintained a certain distance from Adams.

A Second Term for Washington and Adams

August 1790 signaled major changes for the young government. The capital was moved from New York to Philadelphia, where it would remain for ten years.

A new political difficulty also surfaced. Members of Congress had split into factions based on geography or political thinking. One side became known as the Federalists, and the other as the Republicans. Although Adams felt that political parties might ruin the nation, his thinking was more aligned with the Federalists, and he became associated with that party. The political divisions, however, meant difficulties in reaching decisions because each side voted in the interest of its own goals.

★

In December 1790 Congress moved from New York to the temporary capital of Philadelphia.

★

George Washington despised the idea of political subdivisions, especially for the benefit of those involved. To him, the good of the country should have been the only concern for every member of Congress. The bickering between parties became so bad that Washington seriously considered refusing a second term as president.

92

Washington agreed to serve again, however, and he and Adams were elected president and vice president, their second term beginning in February 1793. A monumental event of this term occurred in May 1796, when the United States narrowly avoided a war with England by signing a treaty negotiated by John Jay.

John Adams, President of the United States

As Washington's second term drew to a close, John Adams and Thomas Jefferson faced each other in an election to determine his successor. Adams narrowly defeated Jefferson. By receiving the second-highest number of votes, Jefferson became vice president.

The men were inaugurated on March 4, 1797. Despite their cooling friendship, Adams and Jefferson remained cordial with each other and conducted the business of the nation to the best of their ability.

Relations with France plagued Adams. Angered by the refusal of the United States to side with France in its war against England, the French government granted permission for its ships to raid American merchant ships. American cargo was seized, and American sailors were captured.

In response, Adams built up the army and navy, even though many in government, including Adams, felt that an attack on the United States by France was unlikely. He also appointed three men to negotiate a new treaty with France, but France refused to receive the American envoys. Adams soon felt that France had already declared war on the United States.

Steering Clear of War

Adams did not want war, but his own party, the Federalists, favored it. Adams discovered that some individuals were profiting from the threat of war through their family businesses. The idea of promoting a war to increase personal profit disgusted Adams.

In the autumn of 1798 Adams received reliable information that France truly did not wish a war with the United States. On February 18, 1799, he announced that he sought to negotiate with France. The Federalists were furious. Adams fully realized the consequences of his actions—by preventing a war, he probably would not be reelected for a second term as president.

An Unseen Enemy

Shortly after diplomats left for France in November 1799, Adams requested that the American military be reduced—with the threat of war virtually gone, he wished to spare taxpayers the expense of a large army. With this action, as well as the negotiations with France, John Adams unknowingly angered Alexander Hamilton. Hamilton, who served under Washington as a captain in the Continental army and as Washington's secretary of the treasury, had hoped for a new war so he could rise to glory. By preventing a war, Adams all but ruined his schemes.

Hamilton, a Federalist, had found ways to manipulate members of government for his own benefit. Late in 1799, John Adams discovered that two of his advisers were secretly taking directions from Hamilton. After evidence mounted against the two men, Adams asked for their resignations in May 1800. One resigned, but the other refused. Adams fired the man the next day.

Hamilton felt personally assaulted by Adams. In the summer of 1800, Hamilton launched an ugly campaign against Adams to prevent his reelection, and instead endorsed Charles Pinckney, another Federalist. Hamilton's outright bitterness and open hatred of the president, however, damaged his own reputation as much as it harmed Adams. His attacks on Adams resulted in a split of the Federalist vote. More votes were cast for Thomas Jefferson and Aaron Burr, the Republican candidates.

The New Capital

During the spring and summer of 1800, the United States government was moved to its new, permanent home on a site called Federal City. It would eventually be called Washington, District of Columbia. John Adams moved into the President's House on November 1, 1800. Later that month, Congress met for the first time in the unfinished Capitol. The president and the Congress had, only a few weeks earlier, received word that the peace treaty with France had been successful and a war had been avoided.

December, however, brought bitter news to the president. John and Abigail Adams learned that their son Charles had died at his sister's home in

★

In 1800 the estimated population of the United States was 5.3 million.

★

95

The Nation's Capital

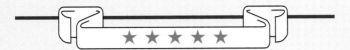

The first capital of the United States of America was New York City. Congress convened there for a few months in 1789, then moved to Philadelphia for ten years.

In December 1790, while George Washington was president, Congress voted that the permanent capital would be an area ten miles square situated on the Potomac River between Maryland and Virginia. Work soon began on the Capitol building, the President's House, and other government buildings. Plans were made for the president and the entire government to move to the new capital sometime in 1800.

The city was in a terrible state when John Adams first visited in June 1800. None of the government buildings were finished. Bricks and lumber were stacked as far as the eye could see. Workmen scurried everywhere, and their tasks made a terrible

Eastchester, New York. Only thirty years old, Charles had been ill for several months. He died as a result of liver failure.

A short time later, the results of the presidential election were announced. John Adams lost to Thomas Jefferson by only eight votes. Adams would remain president until March 4, 1801, the day of Jefferson's inauguration.

John Adams

racket. Adams, who had never owned a slave, was distressed to see hundreds of slaves laboring on the buildings and roads. Despite the chaos, John Adams declared that he looked forward to living in the new city.

When Adams and his wife moved to the President's House in November 1800, it was not yet finished. The yard was a weedy field full of rocks and wagon ruts. Plaster was still wet and the house had only one narrow stairway to the second floor. Abigail Adams used the audience room on the first floor to hang her laundry.

Although John Adams wrote that he enjoyed his time in the President's House, he and his wife did not have the opportunity to live in its full splendor. Adams's presidency ended on March 4, 1801, only four months after he moved in.

A prayer that Adams wrote on his second day in the President's House, which is now called the White House, is inscribed in the mantelpiece of the state dining room. It expresses Adam's wishes for the future of his country: "I pray heaven to bestow the best of blessings on this house and all that shall hereafter inhabit it. May none but honest and wise men ever rule under this roof."

Adams worked to complete all of the business that still demanded his attention, but he did not remain in Washington for Jefferson's inauguration. At four o'clock in the morning on March 4, Adams and two servants met the public stagecoach to begin the journey to Massachusetts. The reason for Adams's early departure without waiting to congratulate his successor is unclear. Historians speculate that he might have been embarrassed, or perhaps he was not invited to the ceremonies. On the other hand, his departure might have been for purely practical reasons. The journey home required that he reach Baltimore, Maryland, before nightfall, and the stagecoach departed before dawn.

Retirement to Quincy

John Adams returned to his home in Braintree (part of which had been renamed Quincy in 1792), intending only to work on his farm. He had made this claim before, but this time, at the estate he named Peacefield, he carried out his plan. John and Abigail Adams happily returned to the habits of a farming couple. Their days were enlivened by frequent visits from their three children, their children's spouses, and especially the Adams grandchildren. Charles's widow, Sally, and her two daughters also moved to Peacefield at the Adams's invitation.

Adams spent his time making improvements to the farm and reading. He also resumed writing letters to relatives and old friends, including Thomas Jefferson. The two had not

In 1825, soon after Adams celebrated his ninetieth birthday, his son John Quincy (pictured) became the sixth president of the United States.

communicated in eleven years, but once the pair resumed writing, their correspondence was frequent. During a two-year period, approximately fifty letters passed between the men.

At the encouragement of John Quincy, Adams began to write his autobiography. Although he did not enjoy the work because of some unpleasant memories, he kept at the project to provide a historical record for his children.

The saddest moments in his retirement came with the deaths of the women he loved most. His daughter Nabby, diagnosed with breast cancer, died in 1813 at the age of forty-eight. Abigail Adams, John Adams's wife of fifty-four years, was stricken with typhoid and died in 1818 at the age of seventy-four.

Abigail Adams left behind a legacy of letters that revealed the daily effects of the war on the home front during the American Revolution.

One last piece of public business required the attention of John Adams near the end of his life. In 1820, at the age of eighty-five, Adams was asked to participate in revising the state constitution for the Commonwealth of Massachusetts. He was pleased to accept, although he joked that his age probably made him so silly that he did not have the wisdom to refuse. He received a standing ovation when he arrived at the convention.

The year 1825 brought a great thrill for Adams. That February, John Quincy Adams became the sixth president of the United States. His father was overjoyed but, with his understanding of the stresses of the position, remarked, "No man who ever held the office of President would congratulate a friend on obtaining it."

John Adams and Thomas Jefferson never saw each other after Adams's departure from the capital in 1801, but they remained close friends for the rest of their lives. Their fates were linked one last time, however. On July 4, 1826, the fiftieth anniversary of the signing of the Declaration of Independence, both men passed away at their homes. Both had told their families of their desire to live to see the great anniversary. Jefferson died in the early afternoon, and Adams in the early evening.

The Legacy of a Patriot

Adams made remarkable contributions to his country in his ninety years. He often placed the needs of his country ahead of the needs of his family. One historian has calculated that Adams traveled more miles than any other individual of his time in the service of his country—twenty-nine thousand miles on ships, in carriages, on horseback, and even by mule train.

Adams's greatest desires for his country were always for peace, liberty, happiness, and virtue. A simple statement from a letter written by Adams on July 1, 1776, reveals his eternal wish: "May heaven prosper the newborn republic."

Glossary

boycott Refusing to purchase certain items as a form of protest against their seller or origin.

chapter A written document that defines the rights and responsibilities of a community.

deacon An aide or low-level officer in a church.

embargo A government order that prohibits shipping certain merchandise to specified destinations, often as a protest.

envoy A person delegated by a government to negotiate with a foreign country.

mercenary A soldier who fights in a foreign war in order to receive payment.

Parliament The highest body of legislators in the English government.

patriot A colonial supporter of the fight for independence during the American Revolution.

pseudonym A false name used by an author, sometimes to protect the identity.

registrar A person responsible for keeping records, often in government or schools.

saltbox A two-story house with an attached one-story room and a long, sloping roof.

selectman A member of a board of elected officials responsible for the business of a town.

typhoid A communicable disease that causes headache, diarrhea, fever, and stomach problems.

vanity Excessive pride in oneself.

For More Information

Books

Hakim, Joy. *From Colonies to Country*. New York: Oxford University Press, 2003.

Harness, Cheryl. *The Revolutionary John Adams*. Washington, DC: National Geographic Society, 2003.

Santella, Andrew. *John Adams*. Mankato, MN: Compass Point Books, 2002.

Woronoff, Kristen. *American Inaugurals: The Speeches, the Presidents, and Their Times*. San Diego: Blackbirch Press, 2002.

Websites

Adams National Historical Park (www.nps.gov)
This is the website of the national park that contains John Adams's birthplace; includes maps, photos, and travel guide.

Massachusetts Historical Society (www.masshist.org)
This is the home of the Adams family papers, including the diaries, autobiography, and letters of John Adams.

The Patriot Resource (www.patriotresource.com)
This website is devoted to the American Revolution, with information about documents, battles, people, events, and more.

Index

Independence, 4, 8, 9, 11, 60
  recognition of, 79, 82
  vote for, 63–65
Intolerable Acts, 6

Jay, John, 81, 82, 93
Jefferson, Thomas, 7, 9, 11, 22, 61–62,
  86, 88, 92, 93, 95, 96, 99, 100

King George III, 4, 11, 27, 31, 34,
  35, 37, 48, 51, 56, 63, 86–87

Lee, Richard Henry, 60
Lexington, Battle of, 4, 6, 51–53
Long Island, Battle of, 68–69
Loyalists, 49

Marsh, Joseph, 16–17
Massachusetts, Constitution, 99

Navy, 7, 57
Netherlands, 78–79, 81, 88
New York City, 68–69, 92, 96
"Novanglus," 51

Paine, Robert, 48, 53
Paine, Thomas, 6, 58
peace negotiations, 76–78, 81–83
Philadelphia, 8, 11, 48, 54–55, 72,
  92, 96
political parties, 92
protests, 6, 34, 36, 37, 40, 43, 45

Redcoats, 52
Republicans, 92
riots, 6, 32

Sanctions, 47
Sons of Liberty, 37, 38, 43
Spain, 58, 59
Stamp Act, 5, 32–35, 37, 42, 43
Sugar Act, 32

Taxes, 4, 5, 14, 27, 31, 32, 44, 49
tea, 5, 37, 44–45, 48
thirteen colonies, 4, 8, 10, 26, 53, 57,
  72
Townshend Acts, 5, 36-37
trade, 34, 87
treason, 54
Treaty of Paris, 83, 87, 88

"U," 30, 31
United States of America, 72, 82

Washington, George, 7, 22, 56, 68,
  69, 70, 75
  as commander of Continental army,
  54–55
  as president, 90-92, 96–97
Washington, D.C., 95, 96–97
White House, 97
women, 70, 71

Yorktown, Virginia, 4, 80

John Adams